The Intersection of Technology and Mental Wellness

Explore the Revolutionary Impact of Apps, Virtual Reality, and AI in Enhancing Emotional Well-being

Dr. Joy Miller

Terms and Conditions

Legal Notice

The Publisher has strived to be as accurate and complete as possible in the creation of this report, notwithstanding the fact that he does not warrant or represent at any time that the contents within are accurate due to the rapidly changing nature of the Internet. While all attempts have been made to verify information provided in this publication, the Publisher assumes no responsibility for errors, omissions, or contrary interpretation of the subject matter herein.

Any perceived slights of specific persons, peoples, or organizations are unintentional. In practical advice books, like anything else in life, there are no guarantees of income made. Readers are cautioned to reply on their own judgment about their individual circumstances to act accordingly.

TABLE OF CONTENT

INTRODUCTION 6
   Overview of Technology for Mental Health Treatment 6
   Objectives of the Book 7

CHAPTER 1 10
   The Evolution of Technology in Mental Health 10
   Historical Perspective 10
   From Telemedicine to Mobile Health 11

CHAPTER 2 14
   Understanding Mental Health Apps 14
   Types of Mental Health Apps 14
   Features and Functionalities 16
   User Experience and Design Considerations 17

CHAPTER 3 19
   Pros and Cons of Mental Health Apps 19
   Benefits of Using Mental Health Apps 19
   Limitations and Challenges 20
   Ethical Considerations 21

CHAPTER 4 23
   Current Trends in Mental Health App Development 23
   Personalization and AI Integration 23
   Virtual Reality and Augmented Reality in Mental Health 24
   Blockchain and Data Security 25

CHAPTER 5 27
   The Role of Creators and Evaluators 27
   Who Makes Mental Health Apps? 27
   The Process of Creating a Mental Health App 28

Evaluating the Effectiveness of Mental Health Apps...................... 30
CHAPTER 6... 32
    NIMH's Role in Mental Health Intervention Technology............... 32
    Overview of the NIMH's Research Initiatives 32
    Funding and Support for Technology-Enhanced Interventions 34
    Future Directions in NIMH Research 35
CHAPTER 7... 37
    Finding and Participating in Clinical Trials 37
    The Value of Clinical Trials in Mental Health Technology............ 37
    How to Identify Relevant Clinical Trials 38
    The Procedure for Participating in a Clinical Trial 39
CHAPTER 8... 42
    The Future of Mental Health Treatment with Technology 42
    Emerging Technologies and Their Potential Impact 42
    Ethical and Regulatory Considerations 44
    Role of Healthcare Professionals and Policymakers 45
CHAPTER 9... 47
    Case Studies and Success Stories.. 47
    Examples of Successful Mental Health Apps 47
    Lessons from Real-World Implementations 48
    Impact on Patients and Healthcare Systems..................................... 49
CHAPTER 10... 51
    Recommendations and Best Practices... 51
    Guidelines for Developing Effective Mental Health Apps 51
    Recommendations for Healthcare Providers 53
    Strategies to Engage Users and Ensure Adoption 54

CHAPTER 11 57
   Summary of Key Points 57
   Future Landscape of Mental Health Technology 58
   Final Thoughts and a Call to Action 59
CONCLUSION 61

INTRODUCTION

The introduction of technology into mental health therapy has transformed the way we approach, diagnose, and maintain psychological well-being. This transition is being pushed by the rising frequency of mental health issues, as well as advances in digital technology. The combination of these two disciplines has resulted in innovative solutions that promise to improve the accessibility, efficacy, and customization of mental health care.

Overview of Technology for Mental Health Treatment

The introduction of technology has drastically changed the landscape of mental health therapy. Teletherapy, mobile health applications, virtual reality, and artificial intelligence are just a few instances of technology being used to address mental health issues. These technology solutions not only eliminate geographical boundaries, but also provide real-time assistance, monitoring, and intervention capabilities. For example, mobile health applications offer self-management tools such as mood tracking, mindfulness activities, and cognitive-behavioral treatment approaches.

Virtual reality, on the other hand, provides immersive surroundings for exposure treatment, allowing patients to confront and conquer their anxieties in a controlled and safe setting.

Artificial intelligence is critical in customizing treatment regimens based on the individual's specific demands and habits. Machine learning algorithms can sift through massive volumes of data to find trends, forecast outcomes, and offer specific solutions. This kind of customization is critical in mental health therapy, where a one-size-fits-all approach frequently fails.

Objectives of the Book

The major goal of this book is to give a thorough examination of how technology is being used in the field of mental health care. Its goal is to shine light on the different technological developments that are reshaping the landscape of mental health treatment, as well as to debate the possible advantages and drawbacks of these advances.

One of the primary objectives is to bridge the gap between mental health practitioners and technological specialists.

The book aims to promote collaboration and innovation by fostering a better understanding of the intersection of these two fields. Mental health practitioners must have the knowledge and abilities to properly integrate technology into their practice.

Another important goal is to critically evaluate the evidence supporting the use of technology in mental health treatment. The book will look at the current state of research, highlighting the efficacy of various technological interventions and identifying areas that require further investigation.

Also, the book seeks to address ethical and privacy concerns about the use of technology in mental health care. As digital interventions become more common, it is critical that they are implemented in a way that protects individuals' rights and maintains confidentiality.

This book aims to provide a thorough understanding of the role of technology in mental health treatment, focusing on its potential to improve access, effectiveness, and personalization of care. Its goals include encouraging collaboration between mental health professionals and technology experts, critically evaluating the evidence supporting technological interventions, and addressing ethical and privacy concerns. Through this investigation, the book hopes to contribute to the ongoing evolution of mental health treatment in the digital age.

CHAPTER 1

The Evolution of Technology in Mental Health

The evolution of technology in mental health care demonstrates the unwavering search of improved treatment techniques and a desire to transcend the constraints of existing treatments. This chapter examines the historical context of this transformation, tracing the road from the early days of telemedicine to the current environment dominated by mobile health solutions.

Historical Perspective

The use of technology in mental health treatment dates back to the mid-twentieth century, when telepsychiatry originated as a way to reach patients in remote places. This was a period when the idea of leveraging telecommunications to offer health care was new. The first studies in telepsychiatry used closed-circuit video to conduct therapy sessions, which proved to be effective in overcoming geographical distances and giving access to mental health services for underprivileged communities.

As technology evolved, so did the ways for providing mental health treatment. The 1980s and 1990s witnessed an increase in computer-based therapies, including applications that provided cognitive behavioral therapy (CBT) for a variety of mental health disorders. These computerized CBT programs were among the first to show how technology might be used to provide standardized, evidence-based therapies.

The internet has broadened the potential for technology in mental health. Online therapy platforms emerged, allowing therapists and clients to communicate both synchronously (in real time) and asynchronously (delayed). These platforms introduced a new level of ease and accessibility, allowing people to get therapy in the comfort of their own homes.

From Telemedicine to Mobile Health

The move from telemedicine to mobile health represents a big step forward in the growth of mental health technologies. The growth of smartphones and mobile devices has transformed how mental health treatments are offered and accessed. Mobile health, or mHealth, is the use of mobile devices and wireless technologies to promote health and well-being.

Mobile health applications are becoming increasingly popular, with features ranging from mood tracking and stress management to therapeutic interventions. These applications have the benefit of being more accessible, user-friendly, and frequently less expensive than traditional therapy. They also provide the possibility for real-time monitoring and intervention, which can be very useful in treating diseases like as anxiety and depression.

The advancement of wearable technology has expanded the potential of mobile health. Wearable gadgets, such as fitness trackers and smart watches, can detect physiological signs of mental health, such as heart rate variability and sleep patterns. This information may be utilized to deliver personalized feedback and treatments, making mental health care more proactive and suited to each individual's requirements.

Despite the potential advances in mobile health, there are still hurdles to be overcome. Concerns regarding privacy, data security, and the digital gap pose questions about the fair and ethical adoption of mobile health solutions. Furthermore, the usefulness and clinical validity of many mobile health applications have yet to be thoroughly verified via rigorous scientific study.

The evolution of technology in mental health has been characterized by innovation and transition. From the early days of telepsychiatry to the present era of mobile health, technology has constantly broadened the scope of mental health care. As we move forward, we must manage the hurdles and maximize the promise of technology to increase the accessibility, efficacy, and customization of mental health treatments.

CHAPTER 2

Understanding Mental Health Apps

In the digital era, mental health applications have arisen as a popular tool for those looking for help with their psychological health. These applications provide a variety of functions, from therapeutic interventions to self-monitoring and treatment of mental health disorders. This chapter investigates the many types of mental health applications, their features and functions, and the significance of user experience and design considerations in their development.

Types of Mental Health Apps

Mental health apps may be roughly classified into numerous sorts, each having a distinct goal or treating a particular component of mental health.

1. Self-Help and Psychoeducation App: These applications provide users information and resources on mental health issues, coping tactics, and self-help approaches. They frequently incorporate instructional information, articles, and advice to raise awareness and knowledge of mental health.

2. Symptom Tracking and Monitoring App: These applications are designed to assist users track their mood, symptoms, and triggers, allowing them to monitor their mental health over time. The obtained data may be used to uncover patterns, assess the influence of various activities on mental health, and share findings with healthcare specialists.

3. Therapeutic Intervention App: These applications provide organized therapeutic programs including cognitive behavioral therapy (CBT), mindfulness-based stress reduction (MBSR), and other evidence-based therapies. They intend to give people with tools and practices for managing and improving their mental health.

4. Stress Management and Relaxation App: These applications focus on stress reduction and relaxation, providing users with features such as guided meditations, breathing exercises, and relaxation techniques to help them manage stress and anxiety.

5. Peer Support and Social Networking App: These applications connect users with people who have had similar mental health experiences, allowing them to share tales, offer mutual support, and develop a feeling of community.

Features and Functionalities

Mental health applications provide a diversified set of features and capabilities to fulfill the demands of its users. Some shared traits are:

1. Mood Tracking: Users can record their mood and feelings at various times, gaining insights into mood patterns and swings.

2. Journaling: Provides a platform for users to write about their ideas, feelings, and experiences, which may be a therapeutic activity in and of itself.

3. Goal Setting: Users may create personal objectives for their mental health and measure their progress over time.

4. Reminders and Notifications: Sends reminders for activities, appointments, and medicine to assist users stick to their mental health schedule.

5. Interactive Exercises: Offers interactive activities such as cognitive restructuring exercises, mindfulness practices, and relaxation techniques to help consumers actively participate in their mental health journey.

User Experience and Design Considerations

The UX and design of mental health applications have a significant impact on their efficacy. Well-designed software should be straightforward, easy to use, and accessible to a wide variety of consumers. Key considerations include:

1. Simplicity and Clarity: The app's interface should be simple, with clear instructions and easy navigation so that users can locate and use features without confusion.

2. Personalization: Giving consumers the ability to customize their experience, such as establishing personal objectives or selecting favorite activities, may boost engagement and relevancy.

3. Privacy and Security: Given the sensitivity of mental health data, applications must emphasize user privacy and security, including transparent data handling rules and strong encryption mechanisms.

4. Inclusiveness: Designing with inclusiveness in mind ensures that the app is accessible to users of all abilities, cultural backgrounds, and linguistic preferences.

5. Feedback and Assistance: Including feedback methods and offering access to assistance within the app may improve the user experience and help to resolve any issues quickly.

Understanding mental health applications necessitates a thorough examination of their many forms and functions, as well as the importance of user experience and design. As these applications mature, they have enormous potential to help people manage and improve their mental health. However, their success is contingent on careful design, evidence-based information, and a dedication to user privacy and security.

CHAPTER 3

Pros and Cons of Mental Health Apps

Mental health applications have grown in popularity as a simple and accessible tool for those looking for help with their mental health. While these applications provide several benefits, they also have limitations and ethical issues that users and creators should be aware of. This chapter examines the benefits and drawbacks of mental health applications, offering a balanced perspective on their use.

Benefits of Using Mental Health Apps

One of the most significant benefits of mental health applications is their accessibility. These applications are simple to download and use on smartphones and tablets, allowing anybody with a mobile device to get mental health help. This is especially useful for people who live in distant places or have mobility challenges and may struggle to obtain standard mental health treatments.

Mental health applications provide ease and flexibility. Users may access these applications at any time and from any location, allowing them to manage their mental health around their schedules and requirements. This can be especially beneficial for busy people or those who prefer privacy while dealing with mental health issues.

Another advantage is the possibility of anonymity and privacy. Many mental health applications allow users to seek treatment without disclosing their name, reducing the stigma and embarrassment associated with getting care for mental health disorders.

Mental health applications also have the advantage of being cost-effective. Many applications are free or significantly less expensive than traditional treatment, making mental health care more inexpensive and accessible to a larger spectrum of individuals.

Limitations and Challenges

Despite their benefits, mental health applications do have limitations and issues that must be addressed. One of the most pressing concerns is the quality and efficacy of these apps. There are dozens of mental health applications accessible, and their quality and evidence base might vary greatly.

Users may struggle to determine whether applications are scientifically proven and useful for their unique requirements.

Another disadvantage is the absence of customization in certain mental health applications. While applications can offer basic help and information, they may be unable to personalize their material to each user's specific experiences and requirements. This may restrict the app's efficacy in addressing certain mental health issues.

Privacy and data security are also important considerations. Mental health applications gather sensitive personal information, which increases the risk of data breaches or misuse. Users must be informed of the privacy policies and data security procedures of the applications they use.

Ethical Considerations

The usage of mental health applications brings up various ethical concerns that developers and consumers should be aware of. One of the most pressing ethical concerns is the potential for apps to supplant professional mental health treatment. While apps can be useful for support and self-management, they should not be considered a replacement for professional diagnosis and treatment.

Informed consent is an additional ethical factor. Before utilizing a mental health app, users should understand how their data will be handled, kept, and safeguarded. They should also understand the app's limits and the need of obtaining expert assistance when needed.

The possibility of unforeseen repercussions is also an ethical consideration. For example, software intended to relieve anxiety may mistakenly raise it in some users. Developers must carefully assess the potential consequences of their apps and guarantee that they are rigorously tested and appraised.

Mental health applications have several benefits, including accessibility, convenience, and cost-effectiveness. However, they also have limits and ethical concerns that must be addressed. Users should exercise caution when selecting evidence-based and secure apps, while developers should focus the quality, customization, and ethical implications of their products.

CHAPTER 4

Current Trends in Mental Health App Development

The environment of mental health app development is continually changing, driven by technical breakthroughs and a growing desire for new solutions. This chapter delves into some of the most recent developments in mental health app development, such as customization and AI integration, the usage of virtual and augmented reality (VR/AR), and the use of blockchain technology for data protection.

Personalization and AI Integration

One of the most significant developments in mental health app development is the emphasis on customization and the use of artificial intelligence (AI). Personalization entails adapting the app's content and interventions to each user's specific requirements, preferences, and behavioral patterns. This can considerably improve the app's performance by offering more relevant and focused assistance.

AI is critical to allowing customization. Machine learning algorithms may use user data, such as mood logs, activity levels, and interaction patterns, to find trends and forecast future behavior. This information may then be utilized to tailor the app's recommendations, interventions, and content to each user's specific profile.

AI can improve the app's responsiveness and flexibility. Natural language processing-powered chatbots, for example, can give real-time, interactive help by mimicking a discussion with a mental health practitioner. These AI-powered features have the potential to improve the engagement and effectiveness of mental health apps in offering individualized care.

Virtual Reality and Augmented Reality in Mental Health

VR and augmented reality (AR) are emerging as viable technologies for developing mental health apps. VR immerses the user in a totally virtual environment, whereas AR overlays digital information on the actual world. Both technologies have the potential to revolutionize mental health therapy by delivering immersive, interactive experiences that can mimic real-life scenarios or teach relaxation and mindfulness techniques.

VR is being utilized in mental health for exposure treatment, which involves progressively exposing people to their phobias or triggers in a controlled virtual environment. This is particularly useful for treating phobias, anxiety disorders, and post-traumatic stress disorder (PTSD). VR may also be used to relax and relieve stress by presenting users with pleasant virtual settings to explore and interact with.

In contrast, augmented reality (AR) has the ability to provide real-time support and interventions. When an AR app senses stress or anxiety, it may overlay calming pictures or coping instructions on the user's environment. This can give instant, context-aware assistance to individuals in managing their mental health in everyday situations.

Blockchain and Data Security

With the growing popularity of mental health applications, data security and privacy have become key considerations. Blockchain technology is developing as an option for improving the security and privacy of health data. Blockchain is a decentralized, distributed ledger that securely records transactions between computers. In the context of mental health apps, blockchain may be used to securely store and manage user data, making it tamper-proof and resistant to unwanted access.

By utilizing blockchain, mental health applications can give individuals more control over their data. Users can have a secure, private key to access their data, and they can choose who they share it with. This can boost user trust and desire to use mental health applications since they know their sensitive information is safe.

Personalization, AI integration, the usage of VR and AR, and blockchain implementation for data security are all influencing the development of mental health apps. These developments have the potential to improve the efficacy, engagement, and security of mental health applications, making them more important tools for those seeking help with their mental health.

CHAPTER 5

The Role of Creators and Evaluators

The creation and assessment of mental health applications need a collaborative effort from a variety of stakeholders, with everyone playing an important role in ensuring that these tools are effective, user-friendly, and scientifically validated. This chapter digs into the responsibilities of makers and assessors in the field of mental health applications, emphasizing the wide range of skills necessary to bring these digital solutions to life.

Who Makes Mental Health Apps?

The development of mental health applications is a multidisciplinary undertaking that necessitates the cooperation of experts from numerous domains. This includes:

1. Mental Health Professionals: Psychiatrists, psychologists, and therapists use their clinical knowledge to ensure that the app's content and interventions adhere to accepted therapeutic concepts and practices.

2. Software Developers: They are in charge of creating and building the app, transforming the conceptual design into a practical tool that consumers can engage with.

3. User Experience (UX) Designers: UX designers work to make the app intuitive and interesting, ensuring that it is simple to use and gives a pleasant user experience.

4. Data Scientists: They are responsible for integrating AI and machine learning algorithms, as well as evaluating user data to customize and improve the app's functionality.

5. Researchers: Academics and researchers are participating in studies to assess the app's efficacy and generate data for its therapeutic relevance.

6. Regulatory Experts: Professionals who understand healthcare legislation and data privacy rules verify that the app meets legal and ethical requirements.

The Process of Creating a Mental Health App

There are various steps to developing a mental health app, each of which is crucial to its success.

1. Conceptualization: The process begins with identifying a specific mental health need or gap that the app will solve. This entails talking with mental health specialists and potential users to determine the app's aims and intended audience.

2. Design and Prototyping: UX designers use wireframes and prototypes to illustrate the app's layout and functionality. This stage includes iterative testing and feedback to help develop the design.

3. Development: The app is coded by software engineers, who add features like mood tracking, therapeutic workouts, and AI-powered customization. This step necessitates tight coordination between developers and mental health practitioners to confirm the app's clinical validity.

4. Testing: The software is thoroughly tested to discover and resolve any technical difficulties, ensuring that it is both stable and user-friendly.

5. Evaluation: Before it is released, the app is tested in clinical trials or pilot studies to determine its efficacy and user happiness. This evidence is critical in determining the app's therapeutic efficacy.

6. Launch and Maintenance: After launch, the app requires continuing maintenance to handle any technical difficulties, update content, and incorporate user input.

Evaluating the Effectiveness of Mental Health Apps

Evaluating the success of mental health apps is critical to ensuring that they provide demonstrable benefits to their users. This assessment includes:

1. Clinical Trials: Randomized controlled trials (RCTs) are the gold standard for determining the app's effect on mental health outcomes. These trials test the app's efficacy against conventional therapy or control circumstances.

2. User Feedback: Collecting user Feedback allows us to measure the app's usability, engagement, and perceived advantages. This Feedback can help to shape future enhancements and updates.

3. Data Analysis: Analyzing user data, such as engagement metrics and symptom changes, yields information about the app's real-world effectiveness and usage trends.

4. Independent Reviews: Third-party assessments, such as those done by mental health organizations or app review sites, can give an objective assessment of the app's quality and reliability.

The development and assessment of mental health applications requires a collaborative effort from a wide range of specialists. The development process is extensive, involving thorough planning, design, and testing to verify the app's effectiveness and usability. Evaluating the app's performance is an important step in ensuring that it fulfills its promise to promote mental health and well-being.

CHAPTER 6

NIMH's Role in Mental Health Intervention Technology

The National Institute of Mental Health (NIMH) is crucial in the advancement of mental health intervention technologies. NIMH promotes innovation and guarantees that technologically improved therapies are supported by scientific evidence through its research efforts, funding programs, and future vision. This chapter examines the NIMH's contributions to the creation and assessment of mental health technology.

Overview of the NIMH's Research Initiatives

The NIMH's research programs include a diverse spectrum of studies focused at understanding, treating, and preventing mental diseases. In the field of intervention technology, the NIMH encourages research into the use of digital tools such as mobile applications, online platforms, and wearable technologies to improve mental health outcomes. These efforts concentrate on a few crucial areas:

1. Development and Testing of Digital Therapies: The National Institute of Mental Health (NIMH) sponsors research into the creation and evaluation of digital therapies for diverse mental health problems. This includes applications for mood monitoring, online cognitive-behavioral treatment programs, and virtual reality exposure therapy.

2. Personalization and Precision Medicine: Research initiatives look into how technology may be utilized to adapt therapies to individual requirements, using data analytics and machine learning to customize treatment programs.

3. Accessibility and Dissemination: The National Institute of Mental Health (NIMH) encourages initiatives to make digital mental health resources more accessible, particularly to marginalized groups. This involves research into telepsychiatry, mobile health outreach, and culturally appropriate therapies.

4. Integration with Clinical Care: Research looks into how technology-enhanced therapies might be integrated into traditional mental health care settings to improve continuity of care and patient involvement.

Funding and Support for Technology-Enhanced Interventions

The NIMH offers crucial funding and assistance for the development and assessment of technologically improved mental health therapies. This assistance comes in a variety of forms:

1. Funds and Awards: The NIMH provides research funds to academic institutions, non-profit organizations, and commercial enterprises developing breakthrough mental health technology. These awards cover a wide range of activities, including early-stage development and large-scale clinical studies.

2. Collaborations and Partnerships: The NIMH works with other federal agencies, industry partners, and foreign organizations to share resources and experience in the creation of digital mental health solutions.

3. Training and Capacity Building: The National Institute of Mental Health (NIMH) invests in training programs for researchers and clinicians to increase their skills in digital mental health intervention research and implementation.

4. Dissemination of Findings: The NIMH ensures that the findings of sponsored research are disseminated to the scientific community, mental health practitioners, and the general public, supporting the use of evidence-based digital treatments.

Future Directions in NIMH Research

As technology advances, NIMH's research program adapts to address new challenges and possibilities in mental health intervention technologies. Future directions include:

1. Strengthening the Evidence Foundation: The NIMH wants to increase the evidence foundation for digital mental health therapies by funding rigorous studies that evaluate their efficacy, effectiveness, and mechanisms of action.

2. Improving User-Centered Design: The study will focus on combining user input and human-centered design principles to improve the usability and engagement of digital interventions.

3. Addressing Ethical and Privacy Concerns: The NIMH is dedicated to addressing ethical and privacy concerns about digital mental health technologies, ensuring that treatments are designed and executed with user autonomy and data protection in mind.

4. Leveraging Emerging Technologies: The NIMH will investigate the possibilities of emerging technologies such as artificial intelligence, blockchain, and the Internet of Things to improve mental health intervention technology.

The NIMH's role in mental health intervention technology is broad, including research efforts, funding assistance, and a forward-thinking vision. By encouraging innovation and ensuring that digital therapies are based on scientific evidence, the NIMH contributes significantly to the advancement of mental health technology and the improvement of outcomes for people suffering from mental illnesses.

CHAPTER 7

Finding and Participating in Clinical Trials

Clinical trials are critical to the advancement of mental health technologies because they provide the data required to validate the efficacy and safety of new therapies. This chapter discusses the role of clinical trials in mental health technology, how to discover appropriate clinical trials, and how to participate in a clinical study.

The Value of Clinical Trials in Mental Health Technology

Clinical trials are critical for determining the efficacy and safety of mental health technologies including digital treatments, smartphone applications, and wearable gadgets. These studies serve to assess whether a new solution improves mental health outcomes, has any side effects, and compares to existing therapies. Clinical trial data help to build the evidence basis that drives clinical practice and regulatory choices.

Clinical trials can evaluate different elements of mental health technology, such as usability, influence on symptoms and quality of life, and cost-effectiveness. These trials also give information about how different populations respond to the intervention, ensuring that it is successful and accessible to a wide range of people.

How to Identify Relevant Clinical Trials

Finding suitable clinical trials for mental health technologies requires multiple steps:

1. Online Databases: Websites like ClinicalTrials.gov, the World Health Organization's International Clinical studies Registry Platform (ICTRP) and the EU Clinical Trials Register offer searchable databases of current and finished clinical studies globally.

2. Research Institutions and Universities: Clinical trials in mental health technologies are conducted by several academic institutions and research organizations. Their websites frequently include ongoing research and contact information for interested volunteers.

3. Healthcare Providers: Mental health specialists, such as psychiatrists or psychologists, may be aware of current clinical trials and might recommend patients to pertinent research.

4. Patient Advocacy Groups: Organizations that support people with specific mental health issues may have information regarding clinical trials for such diseases.

5. Social Media and Online Forums: Online groups and forums focused on mental health issues may exchange information about clinical trials and recruiting possibilities.

The Procedure for Participating in a Clinical Trial

Participating in a clinical trial consists of multiple steps:

1. Eligibility Screening: Interested participants go through an initial screening to see if they satisfy the study's inclusion requirements. This might include a phone interview, an online questionnaire, or an in-person examination.

2. Informed Consent: Eligible participants are given complete information about the study's objective, methods, possible hazards, and benefits. They must give informed permission before participation, stating that they understand the study and agree to engage willingly.

3. Baseline Evaluation: Participants complete a baseline evaluation to gather information about their mental health and other pertinent characteristics. This serves as a reference point for assessing the intervention's effectiveness.

4. Intervention Phase: Participants receive a mental health technology intervention, which may include the use of a smartphone app, wearable device, or other digital tool for certain duration.

5. Follow-Up Assessments: Participants are assessed at several intervals throughout and after the intervention to determine the influence on their mental health outcomes.

6. Data Analysis and Reporting: Researchers examine the acquired data to assess the intervention's efficacy and safety. Results are often published in scientific publications and may be presented at conferences.

7. Compensation and Support: Participants may be compensated for their time and costs. They are also supported and monitored by the research team during the project.

Clinical trials are critical in determining the efficacy and safety of mental health technology. Finding appropriate clinical trials entails checking web databases, consulting healthcare practitioners, and contacting research institutes. Participating in a clinical study involves eligibility screening, informed consent, baseline assessment, intervention, follow-up evaluations, and data analysis. Individuals who participate in clinical trials can help progress mental health technologies while also potentially benefiting from innovative therapies.

CHAPTER 8

The Future of Mental Health Treatment with Technology

The landscape of mental health therapy is changing dramatically, owing to significant technology breakthroughs. This chapter investigates the future of mental health treatment using technology, with an emphasis on new technologies and their potential influence, ethical and regulatory issues, and the role of healthcare professionals and governments in defining this future.

Emerging Technologies and Their Potential Impact

Several developing technologies are set to transform mental health treatment:

1. Artificial Intelligence (AI) and Machine Learning: AI and machine learning algorithms can analyze massive volumes of data to detect trends, forecast results, and tailor treatment approaches. They can improve diagnostic accuracy, boost treatment efficacy, and offer real-time monitoring and assistance.

2. Digital Phenotyping: This technique uses data from smartphones and wearable devices to monitor behavioral patterns and physiological indicators associated with mental health. Digital phenotyping can give insights into an individual's mental state and aid in the early detection of mental health problems.

3. Neurotechnology: Advances in neuroimaging and brain stimulation techniques, such as transcranial magnetic stimulation (TMS) and deep brain stimulation (DBS), provide new treatment options for mental health disorders. These technologies can target particular brain areas implicated in mental diseases, perhaps leading to more effective and tailored therapies.

4. Virtual Reality (VR) and Augmented Reality (AR): These technologies may build immersive therapeutic settings for exposure treatment, social skill training, and stress reduction. They provide a secure and regulated environment in which individuals may address concerns, develop coping skills, and improve relaxation.

These developing technologies have the potential to increase access to mental health care, improve treatment accuracy and efficacy, and empower individuals to take an active part in their mental health management.

Ethical and Regulatory Considerations

The incorporation of technology into mental health therapy poses a number of ethical and regulatory concerns:

1. Privacy and Data Security: Maintaining the confidentiality and security of sensitive mental health data is critical. Ethical principles and strong cybersecurity procedures are required to preserve individuals' privacy and avoid data breaches.

2. Informed Consent: Patients must be fully informed about the use of technology in their treatment, including any potential dangers, benefits, and alternatives. Informed consent is critical for upholding patient autonomy and providing ethical care.

3. Equity and Access: Equal access to technology-based mental health therapies is critical. Efforts must be taken to make these technologies available and accessible to underprivileged communities, particularly those with little technological or digital literacy.

4. Regulatory Oversight: Regulatory frameworks must change to keep up with technological changes. This involves creating guidelines for the creation, assessment, and implementation of technology-based mental health therapies to assure their safety, efficacy, and ethical usage.

Role of Healthcare Professionals and Policymakers

Healthcare professionals and policymakers have an important role in influencing the future of mental health treatment using technology.

1. Adoption and Integration: Healthcare practitioners must have the knowledge and abilities to incorporate technology into their practices. This entails remaining up to date on the newest technical breakthroughs, recognizing their clinical uses, and removing any impediments to adoption.

2. Research and Evaluation: Ongoing research is required to assess the effectiveness of technology-based therapies, establish best practices, and fine-tune treatment strategies. Healthcare practitioners may help with this study by participating in clinical trials and giving their insights.

3. Policy Development: Policymakers must create policies that encourage ethical and fair use of technology in mental health care. This involves sponsoring research, increasing digital literacy, providing access to technology-based therapies, and developing regulatory norms.

The future of mental health care with technology seems bright, with developing technologies providing innovative ways to diagnosis, therapy, and self-management. However, ethical and regulatory concerns must be addressed to guarantee that these improvements are carried out ethically and fairly. Healthcare professionals and politicians have critical roles in steering the development and integration of technology into mental health treatment, ensuring that it is in the best interests of patients and society at large.

CHAPTER 9

Case Studies and Success Stories

The use of technology into mental health therapy has resulted in several success stories, demonstrating the potential of digital interventions to enhance patient outcomes and revolutionize healthcare delivery systems. This chapter includes case studies of effective mental health applications, delves into the lessons learnt from real-world deployments, and considers the impact on patients and healthcare systems.

Examples of Successful Mental Health Apps

1. Headspace: Headspace is a popular mindfulness and meditation software that has been shown to reduce stress, improve attention, and boost general well-being. Its user-friendly layout and compelling content have made it a popular choice among people looking to adopt mindfulness into their daily lives.

2. WoeBot: WoeBot is an AI-powered chatbot that offers cognitive-behavioral therapy (CBT) to users. It has been found to alleviate symptoms of sadness and anxiety by providing individualized, interactive assistance and measuring users' mood and progress over time.

3. PTSD Coach: The U.S. Department of Veterans Affairs created PTSD Coach, an app to help people with post-traumatic stress disorder (PTSD). It offers PTSD information, self-assessment tools, and coping skills, and has proven to be an invaluable resource for soldiers and those suffering with PTSD.

Lessons from Real-World Implementations

Implementing mental health applications in real-world contexts has provided significant insights:

1. User Engagement: Keeping users engaged over time is a regular difficulty. Successful applications frequently include interactive aspects, individualized feedback, and regular updates to keep users motivated and interested.

2. Accessibility and Inclusivity: It is critical to ensure that mental health applications are accessible to a wide range of individuals. This includes creating user-friendly apps for people with different degrees of digital literacy, as well as adapting information to be culturally sensitive and inclusive.

3. Integration with Traditional Care: Apps that enhance rather than replace traditional mental health care are more successful. Integrating digital interventions into current treatment plans can improve continuity of care and give a more comprehensive approach to mental health therapy.

Impact on Patients and Healthcare Systems

Mental health applications have had a huge influence on people and healthcare systems.

1. Improved Access to Care: Mental health apps have increased access to care by offering quick, low-cost interventions to those living in distant places or who experience hurdles to traditional mental health care.

2. Improved Self-Management: These applications enable patients to have an active part in maintaining their mental health. Mood monitoring, goal planning, and self-help tools allow people to measure their progress and use coping skills in their daily lives.

3. Cost-Effectiveness: Digital interventions have the potential to provide cost-effective solutions for healthcare systems. Mental health applications can help reduce the need for in-person visits and provide early intervention, resulting in cost savings and more effective use of healthcare resources.

4. Data-Driven Insights: Mental health app data may give significant insights into population mental health trends, treatment efficacy, and opportunities for mental health service development.

The case studies and success stories of mental health applications demonstrate the transformational power of technology in mental health therapy. Lessons from real-world deployments highlight the significance of user involvement, accessibility, and integration with traditional care. The impact of these applications on patients and healthcare systems demonstrates their use as tools for increasing access to treatment, self-management, and cost-effective interventions. As the field evolves, these success stories provide a basis for future innovation and progress in mental health technology.

CHAPTER 10

Recommendations and Best Practices

To guarantee the efficacy, usability, and uptake of mental health applications, several variables must be carefully considered during the development and deployment process. This chapter includes principles for creating effective mental health applications, advice for healthcare practitioners, and tactics for engaging users and increasing acceptance.

Guidelines for Developing Effective Mental Health Apps

1. Evidence-Based Content: Ensure that the app's content and treatments are supported by scientific research and evidence-based practices. Collaborate with mental health specialists and researchers to create and verify the app's therapeutic components.

2. User-Centered Design: Bring potential users into the design process to better understand their wants, preferences, and difficulties. Incorporate user feedback to build an intuitive, user-friendly design that meets their individual mental health requirements.

3. Privacy and Security: Make user data privacy and security a top priority. Implement strong data security measures, follow applicable standards (such as HIPAA or GDPR), and properly express the app's privacy policy to users.

4. Personalization: Provide individualized features that adjust the app's content and interventions to each user's specific requirements, preferences, and progress. Use algorithms and machine learning to tailor the app's suggestions depending on user data and input.

5. Interoperability: Create an app that integrates effortlessly with other healthcare systems and digital technologies. This can lead to better data sharing, care coordination, and a more holistic approach to mental health treatment.

6. Accessibility: Make sure the app is accessible to a wide range of users, including those with impairments or little digital literacy. Consider language alternatives, cultural sensitivities, and different levels of technology accessibility.

7. Continuous Evaluation and Improvement: Regularly review the app's efficacy, user happiness, and engagement. Use this data to improve and update the app, correcting any bugs and adding new features or content as appropriate.

Recommendations for Healthcare Providers

1. Stay Current: Keep up with the newest innovations in mental health technology and evidence-based digital therapies. This information can help with treatment suggestions and the incorporation of applications into clinical practice.

2. Evaluate Suitability: Determine if mental health applications are appropriate for particular patients based on their unique requirements, preferences, and technical skills. Consider the patient's health, treatment objectives, and availability to technology.

3. Guide App Selection: Assist patients in navigating the wide world of mental health applications by recommending credible, evidence-based solutions. Provide instructions about how to utilize the app successfully as part of their treatment plan.

4. Track Progress: Encourage patients to share data from the app during sessions. Use this data to track their progress, modify therapy programs, and offer feedback.

5. Address Barriers: Collaborate with patients to identify and resolve any obstacles to utilizing mental health applications, such as technical challenges, privacy concerns, or a lack of desire.

Strategies to Engage Users and Ensure Adoption

1. User Engagement: Make the app entertaining and motivational. Incorporate interactive components, gamification, and prizes to encourage frequent use and long-term engagement.

2. Onboarding Experience: Create a smooth onboarding process that walks users through the app's features and functions. Clear instructions and tutorials may help users get started and learn how to use the program efficiently.

3. Social Support: Include elements like community forums or peer support networks to help people feel connected and share their experiences.

4. Feedback Mechanisms: Implement feedback methods to allow users to submit feedback on their app experience. Use this input to create continual changes and respond to user requirements.

5. Marketing and Awareness: Create a marketing and awareness campaign to promote the app and inform potential users of its benefits. Work with mental health organizations, healthcare providers, and advocacy groups to reach a larger audience.

6. Training and Support: Provide users with training and support tools to assist them use the app and resolve any difficulties. Provide easily accessible customer service channels so that people may seek assistance as needed.

Creating and deploying effective mental health applications necessitates a multidimensional strategy that includes evidence-based content, user-centered design, privacy and security, and continuous review. Healthcare practitioners play an important role in assisting patients through the selection and usage of these applications. To engage users and ensure adoption, provide a stimulating and helpful user experience, provide simple onboarding and feedback methods, and raise app awareness and support. By following these suggestions and best practices, developers and healthcare practitioners may help mental health applications succeed and have a positive influence on mental health and healthcare outcomes.

CHAPTER 11

Summary of Key Points

Several crucial elements have surfaced as we investigate mental health technologies. For starters, incorporating technology into mental health care has the potential to transform treatment accessibility, efficacy, and customization. Mental health applications, teletherapy, virtual reality, and artificial intelligence are just a handful of the technologies that are changing the way we view mental health.

Effective mental health applications require a multidisciplinary strategy that includes mental health specialists, software engineers, user experience designers, and data scientists. These apps must be evidence-based, emphasize user privacy and security, and be tailored to the user's specific requirements and preferences.

Clinical trials are vital in determining the efficacy and safety of mental health technology. Participation in these studies is critical to furthering our understanding of how technology may best be used to assist mental health.

The future of mental health technology seems hopeful, with emerging technologies such as digital phenotyping, neurotechnology, and blockchain providing new paths for therapy and study. However, this future presents ethical and regulatory challenges that must be addressed in order to ensure that technology is utilized responsibly and fairly.

Future Landscape of Mental Health Technology

Several themes are expected to define the future of mental health technology. Personalization and precision medicine will become increasingly crucial as AI and machine learning allow for more targeted and adaptable therapies. Digital phenotyping and wearable technology will give real-time monitoring and insights into an individual's mental state, enabling earlier intervention and more proactive mental health care.

Collaboration among healthcare practitioners, technology developers, academics, and policymakers is critical to the successful integration of technology into mental health treatment. Interoperability of various technologies and healthcare systems will be critical for providing smooth and comprehensive treatment.

As technology advances, there will be an increased need for continuous study and assessment to ensure that innovative solutions are safe, effective, and ethical. Regulatory frameworks will need to evolve to keep up with technology improvements while still protecting individuals' rights and privacy.

Final Thoughts and a Call to Action

The use of technology into mental health treatment has enormous potential to enhance the lives of people with mental illnesses. However, fulfilling this promise would need a collaborative effort from all parties involved in mental health treatment and technological development.

A call to action has been issued for mental health practitioners to embrace technology as a tool for improving treatment, as well as for technology developers to consider user requirements and well-being in their designs.

Researchers must continue to thoroughly assess the effectiveness of mental health devices, and legislators must guarantee that rules promote innovation while respecting individuals' privacy and rights.

Collaboration and conversation among all stakeholders are critical for managing the difficulties and possibilities posed by mental health technology. Working together, we can use technology to make mental health treatment more accessible, effective, and tailored for everyone.

The evolution of mental health technology is continual, with each innovation bringing new opportunities and difficulties. As we move forward, it is critical that we maintain individuals' well-being at the forefront of our efforts, ensuring that technology is used to empower people and effect positive change in the field of mental health.

CONCLUSION

As we conclude our investigation of the junction of technology and mental health, it is evident that we are on the verge of a new era in mental health treatment. Advancements in digital technology, ranging from smartphone applications to virtual reality, have created unprecedented prospects to improve the accessibility, customization, and efficacy of mental health therapies.

This book has explored the landscape of mental health technology, providing light on the critical role of developers, healthcare professionals, and legislators in crafting a future in which technology may be a strong ally in the goal of mental well-being.

The journey through this book has highlighted the transforming power of mental health applications, which provide a variety of tools for self-management, treatment, and support. We discussed the vital need of designing these applications using evidence-based techniques, ensuring they are user-centered, and prioritizing users' privacy and security.

The investigation of clinical trials showed their critical role in confirming the efficacy of digital therapies, ensuring that the technologies we use are not just creative but also scientifically sound.

The future landscape of mental health technology is one of great promise, with emerging technologies such as artificial intelligence, digital phenotyping, and blockchain ready to push the frontiers of what is possible in mental health treatment. These improvements point to a future in which therapies are not just reactive but also proactive, allowing for hitherto inconceivable early diagnosis and intervention.

However, the future is not without its obstacles. As we strive to strike a delicate balance between innovation and the preservation of individual rights and privacy, ethical and regulatory issues become increasingly important. Healthcare professionals and politicians play an increasingly important role in directing the ethical, egalitarian, and successful integration of technology into mental health treatment.

As we get to the end of our trip, we must remember that incorporating technology into mental health treatment is really a means to a goal. The ultimate objective is to enhance the lives of those dealing with mental health challenges by giving them the skills and support they require to flourish. This book has set forth the foundations, problems, and potential of mental health technology, but it is up to each of us to put these ideas into practice.

The call to action for developers and innovators is to keep pushing the frontiers of what is possible while always prioritizing user well-being in your designs. Healthcare practitioners should embrace these new tools as part of their arsenal while assisting their patients, while also pushing for the continuous development and review of these technologies. The politicians' goal is to establish an atmosphere that encourages innovation while protecting individuals' safety, privacy, and rights.

And to you, the reader, whether you are a mental health professional, a technology enthusiast, or someone interested in the future of mental health care, the call to action is to engage with these technologies, to learn, to explore, and to help shape a future in which mental health is not a challenge to be overcome, but rather a pillar of a fulfilling and empowered life.

We are all on the same road with mental health technology. It is a voyage of invention, obstacles, and limitless possibility. Let us go forward with a sense of purpose, a dedication to ethical standards, and a vision of a future in which technology and mental health care merge to create a world of better knowledge, support, and well-being for everyone.

Printed in Great Britain
by Amazon